EGYPT

Julie Murray

Big Buddy BOOKS
Explore the Countries

VISIT US AT
www.abdopublishing.com

Published by ABDO Publishing Company, PO Box 398166, Minneapolis, MN 55439.

Printed in the United States of America, North Mankato, Minnesota.
042013
092013

♻ PRINTED ON RECYCLED PAPER

Coordinating Series Editor: Rochelle Baltzer
Editor: Sarah Tieck
Contributing Editors: Megan M. Gunderson, Marcia Zappa
Graphic Design: Adam Craven
Cover Photograph: *Shutterstock*: sculpies.
Interior Photographs/Illustrations: *Alamy*: Aroon Vater (p. 9); *AP Photo*: AP Photo (p. 15), Amr Nabil (p. 19), North Wind Picture Archives via AP Images (p. 13); *Getty Images*: Fred Bruemmer (p. 21), KARIM JAAFAR/AFP (p. 35), Ritterbach Ritterbach (p. 34); *Glow Images*: © Eye Ubiquitous (p. 25), Franz Marc Frei/LOOK-foto (p. 29), Insights (p. 31), The Print Collector (p. 33), ARCO/P. Schickert (p. 27), Arco/F. Schneider (p. 27), SuperStock (pp. 13, 31), Werner Forman Archive (p. 16); *iStockphoto*: ©iStockphoto.com/opulent-images (p. 34), ©iStockphoto.com/PeskyMonkey (p. 37); *Photo Researchers, Inc.*: M. Phillip Kahl/Science Source (p. 23); *Shutterstock*: Antonio Abrignani (p. 17), Baloncici (p. 38), Barbara Barbour (p. 11), Bzzuspajk (p. 9), Iakov Filimonov (pp. 19, 38), javarman (p. 11), Pius Lee (p. 5), Mikhail Nekrasov (p. 35), WitR (p. 35).

Country population and area figures taken from the CIA World Factbook.

Library of Congress Control Number: 2013932175

Cataloging-in-Publication Data

Murray, Julie.
Egypt / Julie Murray.
  p. cm. -- (Explore the countries)
ISBN 978-1-61783-809-5 (lib. bdg.)
1. Egypt--Juvenile literature.   I. Title.
962--dc23

2013932175

EGYPT

Contents

Around the World

Our world has many countries. Each country has different land. It has its own rich history. And, the people have their own languages and ways of life.

Egypt is a country in both Africa and Asia. What do you know about Egypt? Let's learn more about this place and its story!

Did You Know?

Arabic is the official language of Egypt. The words are written using the Arabic alphabet.

The famous Great Sphinx and Pyramids of Giza are in northern Egypt. They are thousands of years old!

PASSPORT TO EGYPT

Most of Egypt is in Africa. But a small part called the Sinai **Peninsula** is in Asia. The Gaza Strip, Israel, Sudan, and Libya border Egypt. The Mediterranean Sea is north. The Red Sea forms most of the eastern border.

Egypt's total area is 386,662 square miles (1,001,450 sq km). It has the third-largest population in Africa! About 83.7 million people live there.

SAY IT

Sinai
SEYE-neye

WHERE IN THE WORLD?

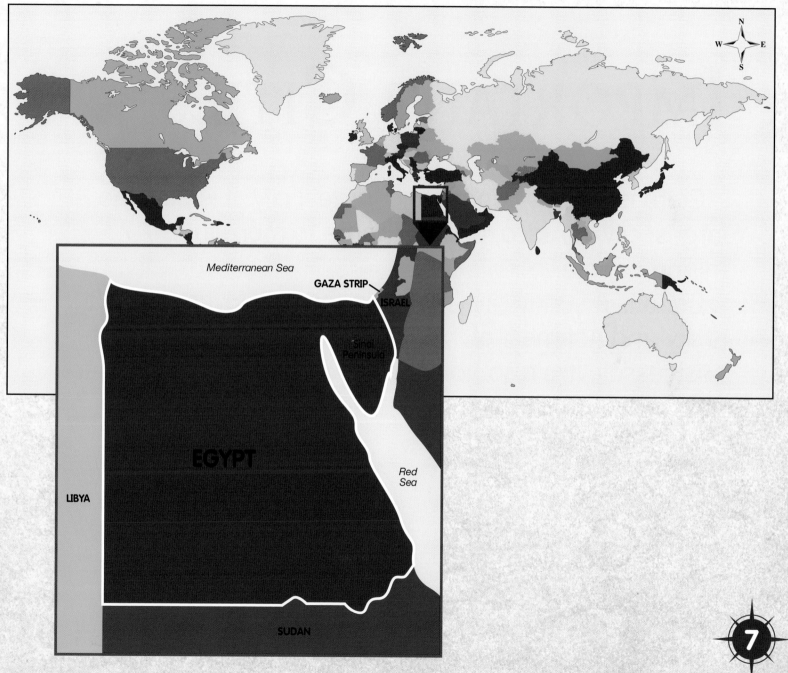

Mediterranean Sea

GAZA STRIP

ISRAEL

Sinai Peninsula

EGYPT

Red Sea

LIBYA

SUDAN

IMPORTANT CITIES

Cairo is Egypt's **capital** and largest city. It is also the largest city in Africa. Cairo is home to more than 7.7 million people.

Cairo is a sunny city located in the Nile River valley. It is dry and hot most of the year. The city has important businesses. It is also home to the Mugamma and other government buildings.

SAY IT

Cairo
KEYE-roh

Did You Know?

Cairo only receives about one inch (2.5 cm) of rain each year.

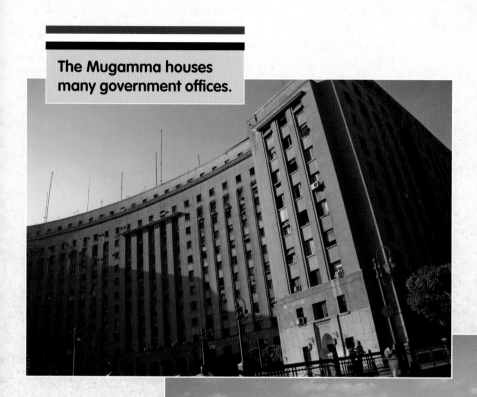

The Mugamma houses many government offices.

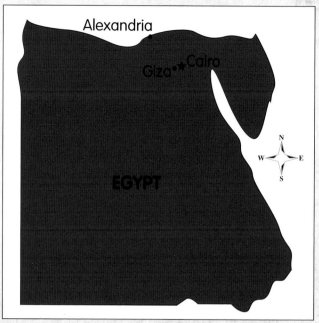

EGYPT

Alexandria

Giza ★ Cairo

The Nile River flows north through Cairo. It is the world's longest river.

Alexandria is Egypt's second-largest city. More than 4.1 million people live there. This busy port has been around for more than 2,000 years. It is located on the Mediterranean Sea.

Giza is Egypt's third-largest city, with more than 2.6 million people. It is part of the Cairo **metropolitan** area. Giza is home to the famous Pyramids of Giza.

SAY IT

Alexandria
a-lihg-ZAN-dree-uh

Giza
GEE-zuh

Many visitors spend time at Alexandria's beaches. The Corniche is a road along the shoreline.

Some people come to Egypt just to see the Pyramids of Giza.

EGYPT IN HISTORY

Egypt was one of the first **civilizations**. Ancient Egypt was ruled by **pharaohs** for about 3,000 years. Egyptians made amazing advancements during that time. They built the Pyramids of Giza!

Around 640, Egypt became part of the **Islamic** Empire. In 1250, a military group called the Mamluks took control. They ruled for more than 200 years. During this time, Egyptians made important accomplishments in building, art, and writing.

Did You Know?

Ancient Egyptians made the first national government. And, they created a basic math system and a 365-day calendar. They also made a type of paper from papyrus plants.

In ancient Egypt, words were carved in stone using hieroglyphics. This form of writing uses pictures instead of letters.

SAY IT

hieroglyphic
heye-uh-ruh-GLIH-fihk

Ancient Egyptians first settled near the Nile River. The people called this area *Kemet*. They used the Nile for water and travel.

13

Over the years, outside forces continued to invade Egypt. In 1805, Muhammad 'Ali took control of Egypt. In the late 1800s, the area and its trading routes were controlled by the British. In 1922, Egypt gained its independence.

Egypt's government and leaders have changed several times since 1922. In 2011, President Hosni Mubarak stepped down. A new group took control of Egypt. In 2012, they began to work on writing their rules and laws.

Anwar el-Sadat became Egypt's president in 1970. He is known for his efforts to make peace between Egypt and Israel.

15

Timeline

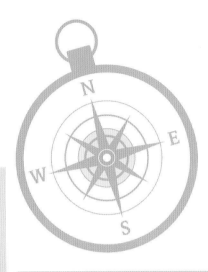

1171 AD

Saladin became Egypt's ruler. He brought the Sunni **Islam** religion back. He also helped Egypt grow in power.

About 2500 BC

Ancient Egyptians built the Great Pyramid of Giza.

About 1340 BC

Sculptor Thutmose made a bust of Egyptian queen Nefertiti. Her face looks very real, which is unusual for art from that time. Later it became famous and was copied by other artists.

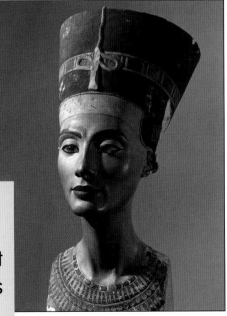

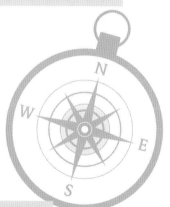

1869

The Suez Canal was completed. This waterway connects the Mediterranean Sea with the Red Sea. It shortened travel time for ships.

1922

The tomb of **Pharaoh** Tutankhamen, or King Tut, was located. Inside, scientists found gold and art. People around the world became interested in King Tut and ancient Egypt.

2011

A new government took over Egypt. The next year, leaders began to write a new set of laws for the people to vote on.

An Important Symbol

Egypt's flag was adopted in 1984. It has red, white, and black stripes. The Eagle of Saladin is in the center. It is also Egypt's coat of arms.

Egypt's government is a **republic**. The president is the head of state. The prime minister is the head of government. Laws are made by the House of Representatives.

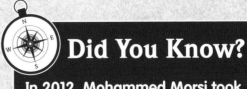

Did You Know?

In 2012, Mohammed Morsi took office as Egypt's president.

In 2011, different groups fought to control Egypt's government.

Many people believe the Eagle of Saladin stands for power, beauty, and independence.

19

ACROSS THE LAND

Egypt is known for its deserts. Deserts cover more than half of the country. The Arabian Desert is in the east. The Libyan Desert is west.

The Nile River flows through Egypt for about 1,000 miles (1,600 km). It drains into the Mediterranean Sea. There, it forms a **delta**.

The Sinai **Peninsula** is east of the Suez Canal. Its land is rich in oil. It also has Egypt's highest point, Mount Katrina.

An oasis is an area in the desert where underground water comes to the surface. This allows plants to grow.

Many types of animals make their homes in Egypt. These include camels, ibexes, crocodiles, frogs, and lizards.

Egypt's land is home to many different plants. These include palm trees, papyruses, and lotuses.

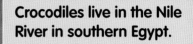

Crocodiles live in the Nile River in southern Egypt.

EARNING A LIVING

Egypt has important businesses. Many are controlled by the government. The country's factories make food, cloth, and cement. Many people work in service jobs, such as helping visitors.

Natural **resources** are found in Egypt. These include oil and natural gas. Farmers grow cotton, eggplants, figs, and other produce. Goats and sheep are among the livestock raised there.

Many farms are in the rich Nile River and delta. Thousands of years of the flooding has created good farmland.

LIFE IN EGYPT

Egypt is known for its history. There are pyramids and other historic places. But, the country also has modern cities.

A popular meal in Egypt is bread dipped in vegetable soup. Tea and coffee are favorite drinks. Milk often comes from sheep and goats. The wealthy can afford a variety of meats, fruits, and vegetables.

 Did You Know?

In Egypt, children begin school at age 6. The law says they must attend school until age 14.

Many Muslim Egyptian women cover their hair, ears, and arms. Men may wear skullcaps and grow beards.

Egyptians called Bedouins move around in deserts. They have herds of camels, goats, and sheep.

Egyptians enjoy shopping and spending time with each other. They often go to outdoor markets called souks.

Religion is very important in Egypt. About 90 percent of Egyptians practice **Islam**. Most follow the Sunni branch. They pray five times each day. They also **fast** and give money to the poor. Many attend Muslim festivals during the year.

SAY IT

souk
SOOK

Al-Azhar mosque was the first mosque in Cairo. It was founded in 970.

Famous Faces

Egypt's history is full of strong leaders. Ramses III was a **pharaoh** of ancient Egypt. His birthdate is not known. He ruled from about 1187 BC until his death in about 1156 BC.

Ramses III was a powerful leader. During his rule, Egypt fought in three wars. He led the military and kept invaders out of his country.

The memorial temple of Ramses III (*above*) is near the famous Valley of the Kings. It is decorated with hieroglyphs (*below*).

Cleopatra was a famous queen of Egypt. She lived from 69 to 30 BC. Cleopatra was known for her beauty and power.

Cleopatra lived in Alexandria. She also spent time in Rome. Her son with famous Roman ruler Julius Caesar became one of Egypt's kings. She later married Roman ruler Mark Antony. They joined together to try to keep their kingdoms safe and strong.

Did You Know?

Famous writers such as William Shakespeare have told Cleopatra's life story.

Ancient Egyptians carved images of Cleopatra and her son Caesarion.

Tour Book

Have you ever been to Egypt? If you visit the country, here are some places to go and things to do!

 ## See

Visit the Valley of the Kings near Luxor. The tombs of more than 60 kings have been found there. Inside them are carvings, paintings, and hieroglyphs.

 ## Eat

Taste different foods at a souk. You'll find people drinking tea or coffee and spending time with friends. Try a fig or a dip called *dukkah*!

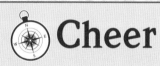 Learn

Wander through Cairo's Egyptian Museum.
There is a room filled with mummies.
And, there are treasures from King Tut's tomb!

Cheer

Watch a soccer game. This sport is very
popular in Egypt. Egyptians cheer for their
favorite teams on television and go to matches.

Explore

Travel on the Nile River. Many people
tour Egypt's famous places by boat.

A Great Country

The story of Egypt is important to our world. The people and places that make up this country offer something special. They help make the world a more beautiful, interesting place.

Camels are common in Egypt. People may raise them or use them for work. They are often found in areas popular with visitors.

Egypt Up Close

Official Name: Arab Republic of Egypt

Flag:

Population (rank): 83,688,164
(July 2012 est.)
(15th most-populated country)

Total Area (rank): 386,662 square miles
(30th largest country)

Capital: Cairo

Official Language: Arabic

Currency: Egyptian pound

Form of Government: Republic

National Anthem: "Beladi, Beladi"
(My Country, My Country)

Important Words

capital a city where government leaders meet.

civilization a well-organized and advanced society.

delta a triangle-shaped piece of land at the mouth of a river. It is made from mud and sand.

fast to go without eating food.

Islam a religion based on a belief in Allah as God and Muhammad as his prophet. Muslims are people who practice Islam.

metropolitan of or relating to a large city, usually with nearby smaller cities called suburbs.

peninsula land that sticks out into water and is connected to a larger piece of land.

pharaoh (FEHR-oh) a ruler of ancient Egypt.

republic a government in which the people choose the leader.

resource a supply of something useful or valued.

Web Sites

To learn more about Egypt, visit ABDO Publishing Company online. Web sites about Egypt are featured on our Book Links page. These links are routinely monitored and updated to provide the most current information available.

www.abdopublishing.com

Index